The Lighter Side of Educational Leadership

Aaron Bacall

D1407733

CORWIN PRESS, INC.
A Sage Publications Company
Thousand Oaks, California

For information:

Corwin Press, Inc.
A Sage Publications Company
2455 Teller Road
Thousand Oaks, California 91320
E-mail: order@corwinpress.com

Sage Publications Ltd
6 Bonhill Street
London EC2A 4PU
United Kingdom

Sage Publications India Pvt. Ltd.
M-32 Market
Greater Kailash I
New Delhi 110 048 India

Printed in the United States of America

A catalog record for this book is available from the Library of Congress.

ISBN 0-7619-7858-5 (c.)—ISBN 0-7619-7859-3 (p.)

This book is printed on acid-free paper.

02   03   04   05   06   07   7   6   5   4   3   2   1

Acquisitions Editor:	Robb Clouse
Associate Editor:	Kylee Liegl
Editorial Assistant:	Erin Buchanan
Typesetter/Designer:	Larry K. Bramble
Cover Designer:	Michael Dubowe

Introduction

I think of the American educational system as a ship on a life-transforming journey, with the principal at the helm. Certainly, good principals have a clear vision as to where they are headed, and a solid plan for how to get there. They prevent their ship from meandering through uncharted, unpromising waters. The beauty of our educational system is that everyone is welcome aboard the *U.S.S. Education.*

I admire the men and women who are effective administrators of our school system. They have had a remarkable effect on my own life. My parents immigrated to the United States from a small town in a European country since annexed by the former Soviet Union. Each of my parents completed a single year of formal schooling and assimilated slowly to the United States. Very little English was spoken at home. My family was poor with a capital P and my parents depended on the school system to teach me and my siblings to read, write, and do arithmetic. In those days, there were no afterschool tutoring or mentoring programs. However, there were talented, effective school administrators and teachers who accepted the educational challenge and succeeded in educating the youngsters in their charge. The principal was a role model. I recall that she was kind and firm at the same time. She patrolled the halls and I still recall her reassuring pat on my head and that wonderful knowing smile.

I went to school carrying an assortment of advertising flyers, the blank backs of which served as my notebook (as well as my drawing pad).

The teachers were expected to teach me to read and write English as well as do basic arithmetic. Teaching the three R's was the school's core objective and the teachers did this job well. And they succeeded before English as a Second Language programs were ever implemented. The principal steered the ship and the students completed their journey. When I graduated from that elementary school I felt like a "Real American"—truly a tribute to the teachers' hard work and the principal's leadership. To this day, I have tremendous respect for the role that these professionals play in educating our youth.

When I think back to my school days, there are certain things that are highlighted in my memory, and one in particular. I remember a large banner that our principal had displayed in the school auditorium. It read "We Live in Deeds, Not Years." I incorporated that statement into my life, and continue to live by its wisdom today. Perhaps principals never know exactly which of their deeds or actions will make an impact on an impressionable youth. For that reason precisely, a sense of humor and perspective is one of the most important leadership traits a successful principal must possess. After all, the school is a "home away from home" for the students. And a home without humor, a home that is too serious, makes for a stifling atmosphere that can impede both spirit and creativity.

I hope you enjoy the cartoons that follow, and find the nugget of truth that each contains. I like to imagine them being used in front of educators and parents, on overheads, in PowerPoint presentations, during workshops, or in staff development sessions when teachers may appreciate an administrator adding some levity to the long day ahead. If the book sits on your desk alone, or gets passed around among colleagues and friends, I hope you'll find something familiar inside, cartoons and captions that will make you chuckle, laugh out loud, and recognize yourself.

Principals need humor to be effective. And sometimes, they simply need a good laugh.

—Aaron Bacall

About the Author

Aaron Bacall approached cartooning cautiously, stopping at college to pick up a degree in chemistry while drawing cartoons for the college humor magazine, then attending graduate school to pick up degrees in organic chemistry while drawing cartoons as he synthesized glutamate from histidine. All the while he looked for the quirky aspects in all he surveyed. He worked as an antibiotic research chemist and later as a teacher and principal curriculum writer for the New York City Board of Education. He has taught on the high school and college level. He is now a full-time cartoonist and humorous illustrator and is a member of the National Cartoonists Society.

His work has appeared in many publications, including *The New Yorker*, *The Wall Street Journal*, *Barron's*, *Saturday Evening Post*, and *Reader's Digest*.

His business cartoons have been displayed at the World Financial Center in New York City, and in 1977 he was awarded first place for the Best Editorial Cartoon by United Auto Workers.

To my wife Linda,

a very special woman and my inspiration.

I love you.

Aaron and Linda,

who would have thunk it?

To my wonderful son Darron,

how proud I am of you!

To Barbara,

what a wonderful addition to our family!

To Benjamin,

my best buddy and dinosaur guru.

You light up my life. I love you.

To Emily,

my other best buddy and princess doctor.

You light up my life. I love you.

To my Mother,

who smothered me with love.

To my Father,

who worked so hard to provide for us.

I respect and love you both.

The Lighter Side of Educational Leadership

"Take this mission statement back to the committee and tell them to rework it. I'd like it to mention education."

**"I eat an instant breakfast and come to work
on rapid transit, only to be put on hold
by the Board of Education."**

"Here is a printout of the results of our recent standardized tests and here are the same results printed with a very small, hard-to-read font, to make the implications less obvious."

"I have to tell you that your college degree, from the Internet Diploma Mill, raises a red flag."

**"Don't knock it. Since I put the candles up,
the computer hasn't crashed all term."**

"I understand that he was a teacher of English before he got this position."

**"Reading, writing, *and* arithmetic?
Why wasn't I told of this?"**

**"This *is* a novel way to teach math but I'm afraid
we can't try it. It's never been done before."**

"Knowledge is the ultimate weapon. Next!"

"The good news is that all the teachers liked the weekend brainstorming retreat. The bad news is that twelve of them are out today with splitting headaches."

**"Then it's agreed! Our mission statement will be
to deliver more and better education."**

"It's a tough call but I'm going to side with your parents, if for no other reason, because they can sue and you can't."

"The scores for our latest standardized tests are disappointing. We have to articulate a coherent policy of obfuscation."

"Angry parents on lines 1, 2, 3, 4, and 5."

"I know we don't have a formal dress code, but I think you're pushing the envelope, John."

"I connected my food processor to my computer, in case I have to eat my words."

"In a bizarre set of circumstances, the book salesman never showed up, but a drug rep *is* here with samples of Prozac."

**"Before our principal addresses the faculty,
there's something important that has to be said."**

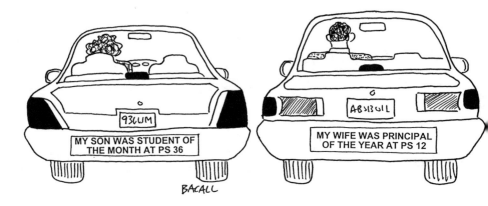

BACALL

"Teaching reading, writing, and arithmetic sounds like a good idea. Let me run it by an educational focus group."

"Ah, the intoxicating smell of freshly photocopied educational surveys ready to be collated, distributed, and discarded."

**"Your opinions are a rephrasing of my opinions.
I like that in a subordinate."**

**"Do you realize that the only change we have had
in this school in the last decade is a change
in our phone number?"**

"Our principal has a sore throat, so she will entertain questions from untenured teachers only."

"As a minimal step toward enabling our school's diverse software applications to interact and share data, I want you to organize a staff seminar on how to turn a computer on."

**"Are you willing to take a drug test and a vow
of chastity while on school property?"**

**"Bugs Bunny, Daffy Duck, Snoopy—
do you have a stamp commemorating
an educational leader?"**

"I wish you would come to me first with your grievances, instead of going directly to the United Nations Committee on Human Rights."

"Your assignment, should you accept, is to increase educational standards while support services dwindle."

"He doesn't do his homework and is disruptive in class. Okay, so what's your point?"

"Being a principal of an inner-city school is a demanding job. My single most important priority is to lower the drop-out rate for students . . . and teachers alike."

"If he starts a sentence with
'Correct me if I'm wrong,'
don't!"

"Ms. Green, I'm reviewing our school's latest standardized test scores. Please send in a grief counselor."

"I hope it's not too much of an inconvenience for you, but I'm desperate to hold on to our good teachers."

**"I was reviewing your school's expanded course
offerings. 'The Poetry of Quantum Mechanics
in the Age of Professional Wrestling'
seems a bit contrived.'**

"We just finished our meeting on raising educational standards. Please call maintenance and have them vacuum up all the educational buzzwords left on the carpeting."

"I was asked to attend a meeting on Accountability in Education. Harold, how long will it take for you to teach me the art of camouflage?"

**"I purchased this great book on time
management, but with my schedule
I don't have the time to read it."**

**"For the next hour, hold all calls.
I'll be practicing tumbling.
I have to learn how to roll with the punches."**

**"Welcome to our staff.
Here's a curriculum guide, a roll book,
and a bag of tricks."**

**"I represent the Student Cafeteria Committee.
With finals coming up, we demand
more fish on the menu. We hear
that's brain food."**

**"The principal will be with you shortly.
He still has a few e-mail jokes to read."**

"Yes, I received the Parents Association's proposal to revamp the school administration. As a matter of fact, I'm passing it around the office as we speak."

**"We've had a total of twenty-seven dropouts
this term. The total is thirty-two
if you count teachers."**

**"Ms. Blumter, please get me a copy of
Educational Leadership for Dummies."**

**"You have reached our 24-hour tech support line.
Please call back at another time.
We are here to serve you 24 hours,
but not in a row."**

**"The legislation HR2109
would increase state aid to education.
Ask not for whom the bell tolls. It tolls for you."**

"What is the meaning of poorly attended staff meetings?"

**"Remarkable! You have the worry lines of
a school administrator half your age."**

**"I'm away from my desk right now.
Please leave a message and I'll get back to you."**

**"He practices the convertible car style
of leadership—top down."**

"It takes a very special administrator to admit he was wrong. So far, I can admit only to being a very special administrator. I'm still working on the second part."

**"The first item on the principal's cabinet agenda
is the high rate of staff absenteeism."**

**"I had my out box fitted with an air bag
in case my ideas crash."**

"The principal is busy right now, so I have to put you on hold. Would you like to hear our mission statement sung by the school chorus?"

"That was a test of our school's emergency broadcasting system. If this were a real emergency, you would have been asked not to speak to reporters."

"Principal Smith, this is a parent of a student in your school. I'd like to discuss my son's grades. Is this a good time?"

**"Yes, I *am* bilingual. I speak English
and Computerese."**

"It *would* be lonely at the top if the phone didn't keep ringing."

**"Were there any new buzzwords created
while I was out to lunch?"**

**EARLY WARNING SIGNS
OF TEACHER BURNOUT**

"It's true that each week you give 100% to your teaching, but you're giving it 20% per day."

"Let's go to our education reporter for more underreporting of school success stories."

**"Ms. Worden, please go to the library stacks
and bring me a few education journals
from the 70s. It seems everything
old is new again."**

"You will be appointed principal of a school and you will resist change for your entire career."

"I have an open-door policy, but only until the air conditioner is repaired."

"Wow! I'd love to get my staff to do that."

**"Al, this is Jack. He's with the Committee
to Eliminate the Board of Education. Jack, this is
Al. He's with the Committee to Increase
Funding for the Board of Education."**

"It's someone from the Society for the Ethical Treatment of Principals asking for a donation."

**"A hacker broke into our computer and,
in an act of random kindness,
organized our student files."**

**"Let's play school. I'll be the principal
and you be the teacher, or you be the principal
and I'll be the superintendent."**

"A restauranteur prepares macaroni and sells it as pasta. I want you to do the same for the educational program at your school."

"Yes, I received the review copy of
***Running a School Is a Snap* that you sent.**
I found it to be a very useful book."

"To maximize classroom instruction, the Feng Shui consultant advises one student desk per classroom."

VLAN
Very Local Area Network

**CORWIN
PRESS**

The Corwin Press logo—a raven striding across an open book—represents the happy union of courage and learning. We are a professional-level publisher of books and journals for K-12 educators, and we are committed to creating and providing resources that embody these qualities. Corwin's motto is "Success for All Learners."